How your body works

What happens when you use your

senses?

Jacqui Bailey

WAYLAND

First published in 2007
by Wayland

Wayland
338 Euston Road
London NW1 3BH

Wayland Australia
Level 17/207 Kent Street
Sydney NSW 2000

Senior Editor: Jennifer Schofield
Consultant: Dr Patricia Macnair
Designer: Phipps Design
Illustrator: Ian Thompson
Picture Researcher: Kathy Lockley
Proofreader: Susie Brooks

Picture acknowledgements
Rolf Adlercreutz/Alamy Images: 17; Apex News & Pictures Agency/Alamy
Images: 26; Jim Craigmyle/Corbis: 11; Dembrinsky Photo Ass/FLPA: 19;
Paul Doyle/Alamy Images: 13; Roy Morsch/Corbis: 7B; Torleif Svensson/
Corbis: 18; Vario Images GmbH & Co KG/Alamy Images: 27; Michael Waine/
Corbis: 14; Onne van der Wal/Corbis: 20; Rob Walls/Alamy Images: Cover, 23
Watts/Wayland Archive: 6, 7T, 10, 21, 24

British Library Cataloguing in Publication Data
   Bailey, Jacqui
   What happens when we use our senses? -
   (How does your body work?)
   1. Senses and sensation - Juvenile literature
   I. Title
   612.8

ISBN: 978 0 7502 5131 0

Printed in China

Wayland is a division of Hachette Children's Books

Contents

What are senses?

You have five main senses – sight, hearing, touch, smell and taste. All of these senses give you information about what is going on in the world around you.

How do you know where you are right now? The answer is easy – you can see where you are. But what if you could not use your eyes to see? You could listen to the sounds around you. You could feel the shapes and surfaces of nearby objects. You might even recognise some smells. You would use your senses.

To listen to your favourite music you need your sense of hearing.

Your senses also help to protect you from harm. For example, your sense of touch lets you know if something is sharp or prickly, or too hot. Your senses of smell and taste tell you if the food you are eating tastes good or has gone off. Your hearing will warn you if there is something loud near you, and your sense of sight will help you to move out of its way.

Your body also has senses that give it information about what is happening inside you. These senses tell you if you are feeling pain, are hot or cold, or feel hungry or thirsty.

When you stand on one leg, your body's sense of balance usually stops you from falling over.

Animal senses

All animals have senses, but they do not all work in the same way. Grasshoppers hear with their front legs, chameleons can see in two different directions at the same time, and snakes smell with their tongues.

Making sense of your senses

Your senses collect information and send it to your brain. Your brain then sorts out the information and decides what to do with it.

Your brain is in the top half of your head. It is soft and spongy and its surface is wrinkled like a walnut. You need your brain for everything you do. You use it to move, think, talk, laugh, solve problems and remember things. Your brain also controls your breathing, your heartbeat and the way your body digests, or breaks down, food.

Without a brain to control it, your body could not do anything, not even breathe.

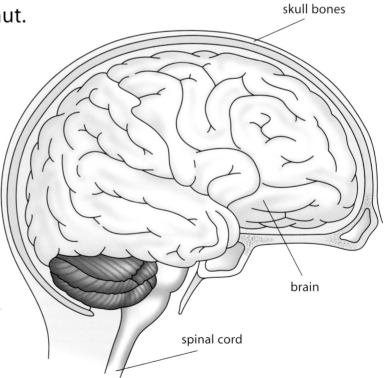

skull bones

brain

spinal cord

Your senses send information to your brain through long, thin fibres called nerves. Nerves connect your brain to almost every bit of your body. Most of the nerves lead to the centre of your body, to a rope-like bundle of nerves inside your spine. This bundle of nerves is the spinal cord. It reaches from the bottom of your spine all the way up to your brain.

Messages from your senses travel to your spinal cord and up to your brain faster than the blink of an eye. At the same time, messages travel down from your brain to your spinal cord and then out to your muscles and other parts of your body, telling them what to do.

Brain box

The hard bones of your skull protect your brain, but even so bumps to the head can damage it. You can help to protect your brain by wearing a helmet when you do activities where you could hit your head.

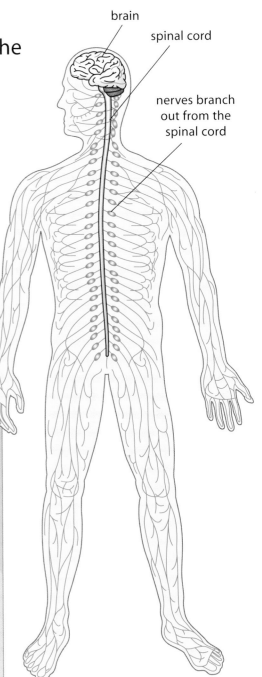

Your brain, spinal cord and nerves together make up your body's nervous system.

brain

spinal cord

nerves branch out from the spinal cord

Looking at your eyes

About two-thirds of all of the information sent to your brain comes from your eyes. Your eyes allow you to see.

Your eyes are like two small cameras. Pictures of everything they see are sent to your brain. Your brain works out what the pictures are and stores them, just as a camera stores photographs.

Look at your eyes in a mirror. Your eyes are two soft balls filled with jelly. Most of your eyeball is inside your head – you see only a small part of it.

The pupil, or dark circular hole at the front of your eye, looks black because no light shines out from your eye.

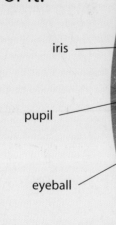

iris

pupil

eyeball

A clear covering called the cornea protects the front of your eyes. In the middle of each eye is a black circle, called a pupil. It is actually a hole that lets light into your eye.

There is a coloured ring around each pupil. This is the iris. You might have blue, brown or green irises. Some people have flecks of other colours in their irises, too.

The irises control how big your pupils are and how much light is let through them. In the dark your pupils get bigger to let in as much light as possible. In bright light they become smaller to stop too much light getting in.

Extra eyes

People who are blind often use guide dogs to help them move around safely. Guide dogs are specially trained. They learn to help their owner walk along streets without bumping into things, cross busy roads, get on and off buses and trains and travel from place to place without hurting themselves.

How do you see?

You see things because light bounces off them into your eyes. This is why you cannot see when it is very dark.

Behind each pupil is a small, soft, rubbery disc called a lens. It picks up the light coming into your eyes and points, or focuses, it onto an area at the back of the eyeball called the retina. The retina sends information about the light to a nerve, which takes it straight to the brain.

The picture the lens focuses on the retina is upside down. Your brain collects this upside-down image and turns it the right way up. It works out what the picture shows and how close or far away it is.

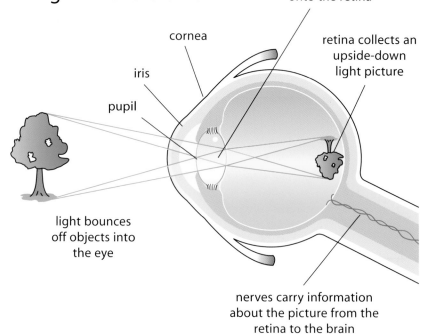

This diagram shows the inside of an eye.

lens points the light onto the retina

cornea

iris

pupil

retina collects an upside-down light picture

light bounces off objects into the eye

nerves carry information about the picture from the retina to the brain

Not everyone's eyes work perfectly. Some people have trouble seeing things that are far away and others have trouble seeing things that are close up. This is because the lenses in their eyes are not focusing the light exactly onto the retina, so the objects they see look blurry. When this happens, people wear glasses or contact lenses to make the objects look clearer.

If you cannot see clearly you may need to wear spectacles, or glasses. It is a good idea to have your eyes tested regularly.

See for yourself

What do you see?

Sometimes your brain becomes confused about what you are seeing. Look at this picture.

Can you see two faces looking at each other? Look again. Can you see an old-fashioned candlestick in the middle of the picture? This sort of picture is called an optical illusion.

How do you hear?

You hear because sounds travel through air and enter your ears.

If you bang on a table top you make the table top shake, or vibrate, for a moment. The vibration spreads out through the air like ripples on a pond when you drop a stone into it. The vibrations are called sound waves. You cannot see them, but when they reach your ears you can hear them.

Sound travels outwards in waves, like the ripples on the surface of water when you drop something into it.

The fleshy, outer part of your ear guides the sound waves through an opening in the middle of your ear into a passage called the ear canal. The end of the canal is covered by a thin piece of skin called the eardrum. The sound waves hit the eardrum and make it vibrate, too.

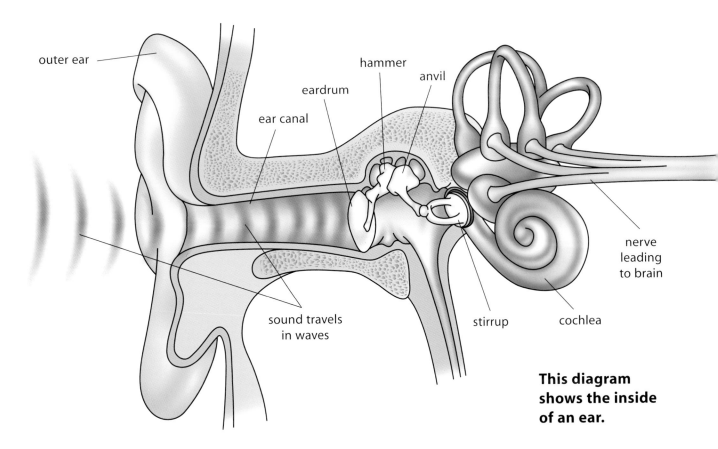

outer ear

hammer

anvil

eardrum

ear canal

nerve leading to brain

sound travels in waves

stirrup

cochlea

This diagram shows the inside of an ear.

The eardrum passes the vibrations on to three tiny bones called the hammer, the anvil and the stirrup. They pass the vibrations into a coiled tube called the cochlea. The cochlea is full of liquid. Thousands of hair-like nerves stick out from the walls of the cochlea into the liquid. The vibrations make the liquid shake. This moves the nerves so that they send signals to the brain. The brain then works out what the signals mean.

Highs and lows

Whether a sound is high or low depends on how many vibrations it gives out in one second. The more vibrations there are, the higher the sound will be. Many animals can hear sounds that are much higher than the ones people hear.

A balancing act

Can you stand on one leg without falling over? If you can it is because your ears are helping you to keep your balance.

On top of the cochlea, deep inside your ear, are three tubes. The tubes form loops called the semi-circular canals. Like the cochlea, these canals are full of liquid and contain hair-like nerve endings.

Every time you move your head, the liquid in the three semi-circular canals moves, too. The moving liquid pushes against the nerve hairs and bends them in a slightly different direction. This sends a signal to your brain so that it can work out what position your head is in.

The semi-circular canals inside your ear help you to keep your balance.

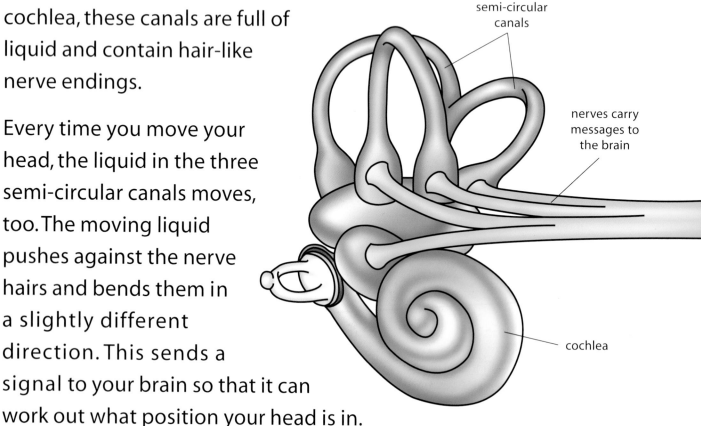

semi-circular canals

nerves carry messages to the brain

cochlea

Your brain also uses information from your eyes to help you balance. This is why it is easier to stand on one leg with your eyes open than with them closed. But your brain can become confused.

If you spin around quickly and then stop, your eyes will tell your brain that you are no longer moving. But the liquid in the semi-circular canals in your ears is still swirling around, and this tells your brain that you are still moving. Your brain gets so muddled it can make you feel dizzy and sick.

People sometimes feel sick in cars because the liquid in their ears picks up the car's movement as it drives along, but their eyes tell their brain that their body is sitting still.

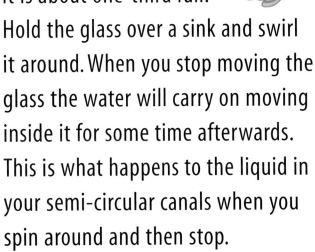

See for yourself

In a spin

Put water in a glass until it is about one-third full. Hold the glass over a sink and swirl it around. When you stop moving the glass the water will carry on moving inside it for some time afterwards. This is what happens to the liquid in your semi-circular canals when you spin around and then stop.

Staying in touch

You are covered from head to toe in skin. Skin holds your body together and gives it shape. It also sends your brain millions of messages every day about how the things around you feel.

Close your eyes. Rub your hands together. Are they hot or cold? Move your hands over your clothes. Are they rough or smooth? Are you standing up or sitting down? Can you feel your feet pressing down onto the floor, or the chair seat pushing into your bottom?

The reason you can feel all these things is because your skin contains millions of tiny nerve endings called receptors. These send information about what you are touching to your brain.

Some areas of your skin have more receptors than others. This makes these parts of your body very sensitive. Your fingertips, lips and tongue are all sensitive areas.

Sensitive snout

The star-nosed mole is blind and uses its nose to feel for food under the ground. It has almost six times as many sense receptors in the feelers on the end of its nose as you have on your hand.

Different types of receptors in your skin tell your brain different things. One type tells your brain if something is hot and another type tells your brain if it is cold. Other receptors tell your brain if a surface is smooth or rough, soft or hard, wet or dry. There are also receptors that tell your brain when something is pressing against your body, and when something is causing you pain.

Millions of nerve endings called receptors lie just under the skin's surface.

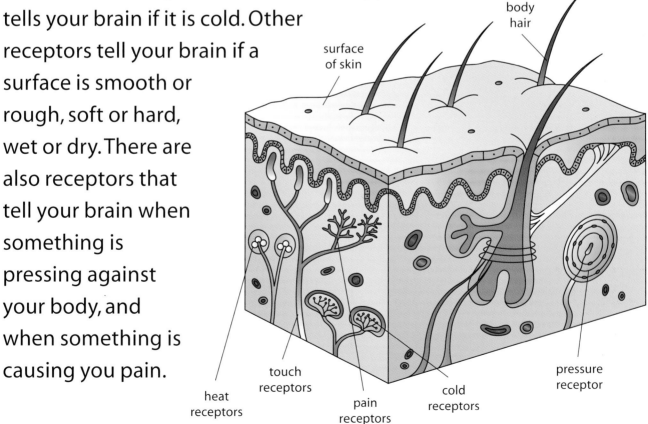

body hair

surface of skin

touch receptors

heat receptors

pain receptors

cold receptors

pressure receptor

Feeling pain

Your body has more pain receptors than any other type of receptor. Feeling pain is one of the best ways your body has of warning you that you are in danger.

Think about what happens if you touch something that is too sharp or too hot. You pull your hand away so fast you do not even know you are doing it until afterwards. This type of movement is called a reflex action.

Reflex actions happen when pain receptors send an urgent message to your spinal cord. Your spinal cord instantly sends a signal to the muscles in your hand, making them pull your hand away from whatever is causing the pain.

Pain receptors in your skin protect you from being burnt by telling you if you are too close to a fire.

Your spinal cord then sends a message to your brain telling it what happened. This is why your brain takes a moment to catch up with what your body has done.

You have pain receptors in other parts of your body as well as in your skin. Your body feels pain when you are ill or something inside you is wrong. It is your body's way of telling you to do something to solve the problem. You should never ignore your body when it is in pain.

Painkillers are made from chemicals that can stop you from feeling pain. They do not cure whatever is causing the pain. Instead they block the messages going from the nerve receptors to the brain.

Pins and needles

If you sit on your feet for too long, they will go numb. The weight of your body is squashing the nerves in your feet and stopping your blood from flowing through them, so they stop working. When you move and let the blood flow back to the nerves they start working again and you get a tingling, prickling feeling in your feet called 'pins and needles'.

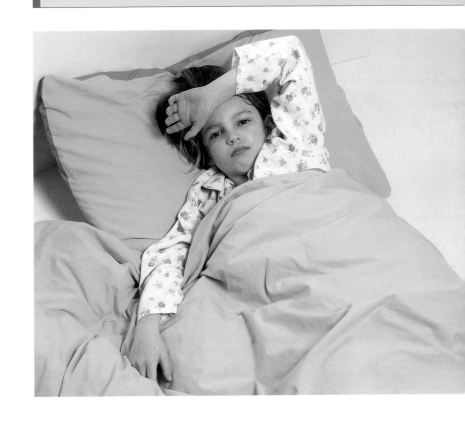

How do you smell?

Smells float in the air. When you breathe in air through your nose, you also breathe in any smells the air is carrying. Your brain then decides what the smells are.

Smells are made of invisibly small bits of chemicals called odour particles. When you breathe in, odour particles in the air are carried up the two holes, or nostrils, in your nose into a large, open space behind them called the nasal cavity.

Smells are carried in the air you breathe in through your nose.

smell receptors

This diagram shows the top of the nasal cavity.

mucus

roof of nasal cavity

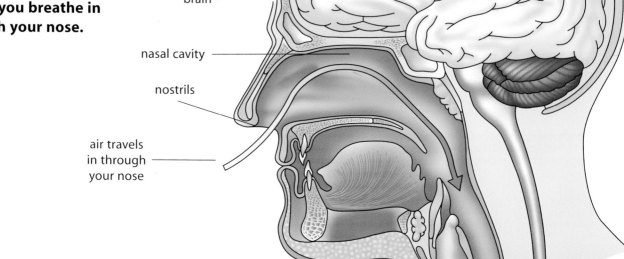

brain

nasal cavity

nostrils

air travels in through your nose

The top of the nasal cavity is lined with a sticky goo called mucus. Tiny hair-like smell receptors hang down into the mucus.

As air travels through the nasal cavity to the lungs, the odour particles get stuck in the mucus and dissolve, like sugar dissolves in tea. The smell receptors soak up the dissolved particles and send information about them to the brain.

The brain uses your memories to help it to recognise different smells. This is how we know that the smell of something burning can mean danger, while the smell of cakes baking is delicious.

Sometimes smells bring back memories of things we have forgotten about. They can even make us feel happy or sad.

See for yourself

Smell test

Ask a friend to put four different pieces of food on separate plates without telling you what they are. Choose foods such as a piece of apple or orange, peeled raw potato or carrot, cheese, or chocolate. Keeping your eyes closed, smell each piece of food in turn and see if you can recognise what it is.

How do you taste?

To taste something you have to put it into your mouth and keep it there for at least a moment or two.

When you put food in your mouth, you use your teeth and your tongue to chew it and roll it around. Your mouth makes a lot of liquid called spit, or saliva. This helps to soften the food and makes it easier to chew. The saliva also dissolves and mixes with chemicals in the food. Taste receptors in your mouth soak up the chemicals in the saliva and send information about them to your brain. Your brain then works out what the taste is.

Most of your taste receptors are in your tongue. Your tongue is covered with small bumps.

Your sense of taste is a mixture of taste and smell. When you chew food, you release odour particles that travel to the back of your mouth and up into your nasal cavity.

Most of your taste buds are in the skin at the bottom of the bumps on your tongue.

Some of the bumps are lined with tiny sack-shaped things called taste buds. The taste receptors are inside the taste buds.

The human tongue has about 10,000 taste buds. Young children have more taste buds than adults, which is why they do not usually like strong-tasting foods. As you grow older some of your taste buds stop working. An elderly person may have only half the taste buds they started out with.

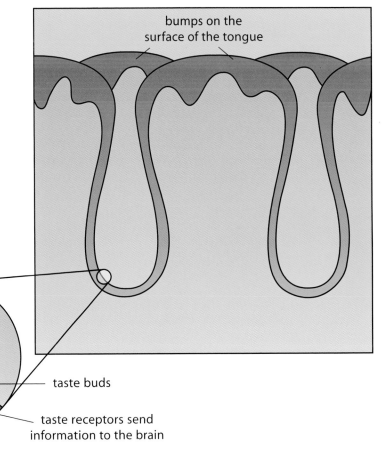

bumps on the surface of the tongue

taste buds

taste receptors send information to the brain

Bad tastes

Your sense of taste does not only help you to enjoy food, it also tells you if something is safe to eat. Berries and plants that are poisonous usually taste bitter, and food that has gone bad tastes sour and horrible. It is best not to eat anything that tastes bad to you.

Taking care of your senses

Your senses help you to enjoy life and they are important to your health and well-being. Try to imagine having no sight, hearing, touch, smell or taste – the world would be a very scary place!

Like the rest of your body, you need to look after your senses. Your eyes can be damaged by strong sunlight, so wear a brimmed hat or sunglasses on very sunny days. Never look directly at the sun. It is a good idea to get your eyes tested regularly, as well.

The sun can burn your skin and seriously damage it. Always protect your skin from strong sunlight by putting on sunblock.

People who work in places where noise levels are high protect their hearing by wearing padded headphones. The headphones block out some of the noise.

Loud sounds can damage your ears, especially if you hear them often. If you listen to music through headphones be careful not to turn up the volume too loud. Also, it is best not to poke things inside your ears, even to clean them. Go to a doctor if your ears feel blocked or if something is stuck inside them.

Be careful when you eat or drink food that is hot. Your tongue is sensitive to taste but not very sensitive to hot and cold, so it is easy to burn your tongue. Burning your tongue is painful and can damage your taste buds. Smoking also damages your taste buds, and weakens your sense of smell.

Resting your brain

Without the information it gets from your senses, your brain would not work very well. But sorting out all of that information is tiring and your brain needs regular rest. When your brain is tired your thoughts get muddled and it is harder to do things. The best way to rest your brain it to get plenty of sleep.

Body words

Words shown in italics, *like this*, are a guide to how a particular word sounds.

Cochlea *(koh-klee-uh)*
A tube inside your ear that looks like a snail's shell. When sound waves reach the cochlea they are turned into signals and sent to the brain.

Cornea *(kor-nee-uh)*
The clear covering that protects the front of the eye.

Digest *(dye-jest)*
The way the body breaks up food so it can use the goodness in the food.

Dissolve
When something mixes into a liquid and becomes part of it.

Ear canal
The open passage that lets sound waves get inside your ear.

Eardrum
A thin piece of skin stretched across the end of the ear canal inside your ear.

Iris *(eye-ris)*
The coloured circle around the pupil. The iris makes the pupil larger or smaller to let in more or less light to the eye.

Lens
A small, clear disc just behind the pupil. It collects the light that comes through the pupil and points, or focuses, it to the back of the eye.

Nasal cavity *(nay-zul kah-vih-tee)*
An open area inside the nose, behind the nostrils. This is where the smell receptors are.

Nerves
Long, thin fibres that carry signals from the senses to the brain and from the brain to all the parts of the body.

Odour particles *(oh-dur par-ti-kuhls)*
Tiny bits of chemicals carried in air. When odour particles get into the nasal cavity they are picked up as smells.

Pupil
The black hole in the middle of each eye that lets light inside the eye.

Receptors
The ends of nerve fibres that pick up information from our senses, which is then sent to the brain.

Reflex action
A movement made by your body before your brain is aware of it, such as the 'jump' your body makes when something suddenly surprises you.

Retina
The area at the back of the eye that sends information about what the eye is seeing along the nerves to the brain.

Saliva
The watery liquid in your mouth that helps to soften food as you chew it and dissolves the taste chemicals in the food.

Semi-circular canals
Three looped tubes that sit on top of the cochlea. They are filled with liquid and help you to keep your balance.

Sound wave
The ripples that travel through air when one object moves against another object. Our ears hear sound waves as different sounds.

Spinal cord
The rope-like bundle of nerves inside your backbone. The spinal cord runs from the bottom of your spine up to your brain and is connected to thousands of smaller nerves spread throughout your body.

Spine
The line of knobbly bones running down the centre of your back. The spine is also called the backbone. Without it you could not stand upright.

Taste buds
Tiny hollow sacks inside the surface of your tongue that contain taste receptors.

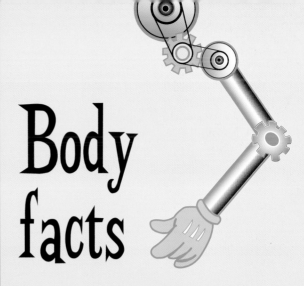

Body facts

- An adult's eyeball is about two-thirds as big as a ping-pong ball.

- Nerve signals can travel at speeds of up to 600 km/h.

- The hammer, anvil and stirrup bones in your ear are the smallest bones in your body.

- The brain can pick out as many as 10,000 different smells.

- Some people have no sense of smell at all – this is known as anosmia.

Index